CW01508194

LOVE IS A FLAMMABLE THING
BY BLAIKE GILLSHAW

2ND EDITION

2022

THANK YOU FOR READING IT.

F.A
B.S
H.S

☆ ☆ ☆ ☆ ☆ ☆ ☆

Half of these poems are about my friends.
I hope you like them as much as I do.

The Girl Who Wore Silk.

I slow danced with you once and I still can't get it out of my head,
I had my hands held on your waist but I followed as you lead.
Your arms rested on my shoulders like the whole world wasn't on them,
But if the world was watching – our careful, clumsy dancing was beyond them.
I felt almost scared to hold you but it also just felt right,
And we did as they do in stories and we danced right through the night.
I closed my eyes for a while and prayed the world had not deceived me,
Because I could not believe how perfect everything seemed to be.

There was no music playing but the silence still felt full.
Neither of us knew what to say, just tried to keep both our minds still.
Then, after a while, you asked if I had danced before,
I knew the answer was no but I said that I couldn't be sure.
See, you gave me butterflies so I couldn't understand,
How familiar it felt to hold you close in both my hands.
It didn't make sense to me how we could feel so scared,
But move so well together and be in a place that seemed to care.

We were in a library, surrounded by old books.
You told me about your family and the way your grandma cooks.
I've never heard anyone string together words,

That sounded so much more like poetry than when I heard your verse.
Your speech held so much gravitas in such pure and gentle phrases,
I never noticed much before how crazy the mundane is.
I found it hard not to look at you in the warmish, golden light,
And I wished for all eternity I could've stayed in that one night.

We danced well into the sunset. Time itself was dancing by.
Before all too much longer, streaks of gold flew through the sky.
We spoke of how we were scared of death. We shared all our other fears.
We laughed it off by telling jokes then wiped away our tears.
The night crept in and cloaked us. Like a film, the scene turned black,
Until everything that had been something turned to myth – no longer fact.
The library was full of stories and just like them were you and I,
A figment of imagination conjured by a mind.

I woke up half remembering, wishing I could travel back.
When I couldn't, I grabbed a pen and tried to fill in all the gaps.
It's true that it's unlikely the smoke and mirrors were ever real,
But I can't explain the feeling that that evening made me feel.
So, if by chance you find yourself in a library after dark,
Dance with the girl who's wearing silk, she'll help you find your heart,
And if by some other extraordinary fate,

You have had that dream, like me, then I promise that I'll wait.

-An artist who awoke alone wishing they could reverse time.

My eyes are heavy,

And my heart is full.

This is how it is,

Supposed to be.

Today the point of life is reading and sleeping and a house that smells like a bakery. Tomorrow it might be 3AMs and chip shop chips and grinning at your friends through tired, blurry eyes. Next week it might be the raincoat you bought at a charity shop on a day that you underestimated the weather. Next month it might be coffee or tumble-dried sheets or watching the rain dance down the window. Yesterday it was the green in the grass and the creases in your shirt and the splashes of sea spray on your face. Last year it was bad dancing and bad haircuts and two years before it was when you finally stopped holding your breath. The point of life isn't that there is just one. The point is that there are hundreds of thousands that might not even last long enough for you to notice them. The point of life isn't one bright spot. It's a sky full of stars waiting to be turned into constellations. It isn't a single mark on a page. It's an empty page that you get to fill. The point of life isn't one single thing. It is everything and nothing all at once.

Huge, cosmic things that nobody understands,
Like falling asleep together and waking up,
Holding hands.

She was gravity.
I felt her even when she wasn't there.

Even the weeds and wildflowers forget to thank the rainfall.

When you walked away,
The sky went from grey to blue.
I could breathe again.

<u>Thinking of you ruins me, every day.</u>

I want for you to call me darling and hold me close as we dance in the rain.
I want to imagine that we are in Paris as we walk down old English cobbled lanes.
I want for you to hold my hand and know that I would hold yours over anything.
I want for you to understand that when I look at you now, it stings.

I see the way that you look at the sky as though everything's broken and dented,
But I see the way that the light hits your eye and, from that? The whole world's reinvented.
I see the way that you look at me and every time that you do I die,
Because I see the way that you get up each day without me and be totally fine.

I know your type and I wish it was me but it's not and that's really okay.
I just wish that it would stop raining; thinking of you ruins me every day.

It is so much easier to be alive in the spring.

Your love is like the sun – safer from a distance.

You feel like you are invisible,
And sometimes you're scared that it's true:
It feels like the world doesn't notice you,
But I hope that you know I do.

So, you fell for the girl as she fell for the boy?

My heart beats and I ignore it.

The grass can be green and you can still hurt inside. The sun is so warm but we still shade our eyes. Sadness and happiness can be suffocating but when you understand them, they are liberating. Life is so short and so terribly long. The flowers all wilt and we blink and we're gone. Feelings are hard but feeling is good so be kind to yourself, the way that you should.

All of the things you forget to write down because they don't feel important or *huge*.
Those are the places that you'll find love.

Little Things To Stay Alive For.

Tying shoelaces, tea and biscuits, hot water bottles, the next season of your favourite TV show, dipping fries in milkshakes, daisy chains, tumble-dried sheets, perfume that reminds you of a friend, lazy mornings, the clouds, fairy lights, cupcakes, handwritten notes, slush puppies, foods that dye your tongue blue, reaching the next level in a video game, finding a new favourite song, roast dinners, jumping in puddles, watching the leaves turn, early nights, late nights, coffee, microwave popcorn, finding lucky pennies, opening mail, birthday candles, laughing, making people laugh, pushing the trolley in a supermarket, dancing badly,

Sometimes.

Sometimes it hurts to be stuck in my head,
Sometimes I'm scared I might rather be dead,
Sometimes alone is the only time I feel at home,
Other times, it's more like a hell.

Sometimes I don't really know who I am,
Sometimes I love that I'm lost.
Sometimes I feel like I'm my only friend,
Sometimes I don't know my own face.

Sometimes too much is not nearly enough,
Other times nothing is the goal.
Sometimes I see god everywhere,
All the time reality's fucked.

Sometimes I'm scared that I'll never be happy,
Sometimes I smile when I'm hurt.
Sometimes I forget that I have a body,
Other times that's all that I know.

Sometimes I see god everywhere.
All the time reality's fucked.

Being stuck in your head is drowning and drought,
Simultaneously.

What I Think About Love.

We want love to fit into our ideologies. We want love to be compatible with the way we make sense of the world. To be explained by science or religion or however you think the universe works. I want love to be complicated and intricate. I love thinking of it as a theoretical thing. I think love is like quantum physics. But I also want it to exist in our world, not just a theoretical state. I want it to be tangible and real. I want a complicated explanation that means soulmates are real and that we are bound by fate. But I don't want that to engulf me. I want it to happen by accident. I want to know someone and realise I've fallen in love with them rather than meet someone with the intention of falling. When I think about love I think about being with that person, walking through the high street somewhere and stopping at a jeweller's to look at rings. And we'd decide just there that we should get them. We'd go inside and choose - either for ourselves or for each other - and then we'd be engaged. And we wouldn't need to get married because the part that matters is the promise to each other and we'd've already done that. And we wouldn't need papers to prove it or trust it. And we wouldn't be cruel enough to make each other stay if the love changed. Love is like the creation of the universe. I guess it is the creation of a universe. But for this analogy, I mean specifically our universe. It happened. It's a fact. You fell in love. But did it happen by accident or by design? Are you lucky or destined? Was it chance or were you always meant to be? I once asked a friend what the point of life was and amongst other things, she said this phrase: 'Everything and Nothing' which is one of my favourite things anyone's ever said. (My Art teacher once told me that blue skies filled with clouds were 'happy skies' and that's my other favourite thing.) I think that's what I want love to be though. Complicated and simple, everything and nothing. I want to get lost in thought about the multiverse and quantum entanglement and I want to be poetic with those theories. I want extended metaphors and rhythm and rhymes but I also want a simple equation that means I don't have to work out the why or the how. One that means I just get to focus on the outcome, on love. I tried to write that equation and I wrote 'Love equals life. Life equals breathing. Breathing equals Carbon Dioxide and Oxygen. Therefore, love equals Carbon Dioxide and Oxygen.' I think that's true. Love is using your life to give to someone else and other people using their life to give to you. It's not an exact science, I know. That would make half of the population trees or something but I'm a writer, not a scientist. But if breathing is science, then talking is poetry and I think that's love. I think that's the point.

Love is quantum physics and poetry.
It's accidental and always going to happen.
It's as unlikely as the creation of the universe and as ordinary as yesterday.

And that? Is what I know about love.

Half of my favourite moments are when I'm alone and the other half are when I am alone with you.

Love Is:

Love is leaving voicemails, knowing they'll be heard,
And memorising coffee orders, verbatim, for word.
Love is half written vows, scribbled down on napkins,
And remembering important things even when distracted.

Love is a family of toothbrushes together, by the sink,
And knowing someone's phone number without having to
think.
Love is fresh flowers on Tuesday and drive-thru meals on
Sunday.
Sometimes you'll find that love is more your friends than it's
your family.

Love is your favourite jumper that you know really is his.
Love is in all of the high fives that you give.
Love is braiding your sister's hair whilst you're watching TV,
And pausing to applaud your brother when he sings to you off
key.

Love is the tumble-dried sheets you sleep in alone,
And thinking of your partner when you smell their cologne.
Love is laughing and crying and living and dying.
Love is everywhere, always. You'll see it, keep trying.

My hands are never still,
Except for when they are holding yours.

My shoes are too tight and my clothes are too big,
And I don't understand this body I'm in.

Even my teeth feel out of place in my mouth.

I don't know you anymore but,
I still think of you sometimes,
And when I talk about you,
I still, call you 'my friend',
And I will do for the rest of my life.

.

Lots of thoughts become sad statements when you think about them.

Will you talk instead, tonight?
I don't want my thoughts anymore.
I want yours.

Things that remind me of my friends.

Dinosaurs, coffee with frothed milk, the colour green, late
night walks, dinner parties, pastel colours, lighthouses, road
trips, meal deals, analogue watches, pistachio ice cream,
varsity jackets, disco-dancing, white wine with ice, floral
prints, frozen grapes, magazines, 3am, empty galleries, copper,
steel, musicals, postcards, water guns, handwritten notes, green
cranes, cowboy hats, ducks, physics, wooden jewellery, film
nights, oranges, second class stamps, baked beans, daisies,
wired headphones, friendship bracelets, cola bottles, titrations,
hockey sticks, cupcakes, netball, bonfires, peace signs, the big
dipper, tennis courts, orange juice, the library, navy blue,
Scotland, citrus fruit, hot pink, basketball, Red Bull, science-
fiction,

The world was pulling him this way and that.
He let out a scream and said "What the hell do you want?"

I burn my tongue on the thought of you.

My Favourite Time.

When the world is unbroken in the morning, I think that is my
favourite time,
Or when you're in my head whilst I'm lying in bed, turning all
of my thoughts into rhymes.
Or just after it's rained in the evening and the road is reflecting
the stars,
And the windows are open and the pubs have just closed, you
can hear the faint noise of the cars.

I like being awake past midnight when the rest of my house is
asleep,
3 a.m, on my own, music playing on my phone when I'm
writing down memories to keep.
Or waking up early on a campsite, with my parents, my
siblings, our dog.
When there's dew on the grass, and coffee in a flask and hills
disappearing under fog.

Or maybe when I'm baking in the kitchen and the house starts
to smell like a store,
Or when I went to see a friend, I hadn't seen since I was ten,
and we ended up talking way past four.
Or maybe when I wake up in the morning with a dream still
fresh in my head,
But maybe one day I'll find this list and say "No, this time is
my favourite…" instead.

We were just kids when we chose each other,
So, I guess it shouldn't be a surprise.
That now that we are grown-ups,
You have changed your mind.

When you eat an orange, you peel it so the rind comes away in one piece. Then you remove all of those tiny white strings and hold each segment to the light before you eat. You asked me, one time, if you think people pay attention to our lives in the same way they would to a film. We concluded that they would if they cared about love because in love, those little things are what's real.

No words can explain you.
I'd know, I've tried.

You put your hand in my pocket and asked me to dance.
I was already falling – now I stood no chance.

Maybe the point of life is the awkward silence between two people who want to be friends.

Cupid Should Warn You.

The hole in my heart that you cut wasn't heart shaped,
Lovers don't take like you did.
You tore into me like a vulture to a carcass,
I still wiped the blood from your lips.

They say that love's torture,
That Cupid should warn you,
That you'll be destroyed if you live.
But there's no way to avoid it:
Love is just pain you forgive.

You watched me bleed out as you cried me a river,
Babe, that's too little too late.
You knew my life like you'd lived it before me,
But my life is not yours to take.

They say that love's torture,
Breathing underwater,
By trying to live, you die.
But there's no way to avoid it:
It's human instinct to try.

I swore love was red like the blood on the floor was,
But love isn't something that bleeds.
I picked up my ribcage and re-tied my heart strings,
And somehow found courage to leave.

Love isn't torture,
It's something much warmer,
I promise, it isn't a myth.

And there's no way to avoid it:
Your life begs to be lived.

This was not the sky; this was my friend,
But perhaps they were not all that different.

We Fell In Love In A Bookstore, We Fell Apart On Our Own.

We used to be star-crossed lovers,
Now we're just mad at each other,
This isn't how the story's supposed to go.

We said we'd die for each other,
Now we just lie to each other,
'Friends to Lovers back to Enemies' trope.

It rained a lot today.
The sky was tired of being pretty.

When I finally said that I loved you, you were too far away to hear me.

And then, something changed.
Now I was moving with time and not watching it pass from the outside.

<u>Playwright.</u>

How many stories get told by the stars?
And when do you think that they'll get to telling ours?
I think I know the ending but I want to read the script.
What if I think we're forever but you think we're a blip?

How can I say "I love you." if I don't know your next line?
How can I pace the story if I don't know the running time?

What if the curtains fall before I've told you how I feel?
What if I am deluded and none of this is real?
If I knew we were fated then I could trust my thoughts,
These wouldn't just be 'pretty words' they would be something
more.

<u>I See You.</u>

You swear that you can see the universe when you close your
eyes at night.
Having paint covered hands is why you're alive.
You're pretty sure that words are your favourite thing,
and you really, really, really, *really* wish you could sing.

You're scared of turning thirty because you're scared you'll
feel alone.
What if your friends start families before you've even found a
home?
You read a lot of books and you feel too much sometimes,
And you don't ever think that you'll get bored of writing
rhymes.

I see you.

Your heart should always be on your mind.

Ghosts aren't real.

You're going to tell me that ghosts aren't real,
As though I don't still feel everything that you made me feel?
As though I don't still get butterflies when I think about your touch?
Or that when I remember the words you spat at me, they don't still hurt just as much?

As though the wish I made on my seventh birthday hasn't changed in any year since?
Or that because you were stung by a bee once at school, when I see one now, I don't still flinch?
As though when I smell *that* perfume, I don't suddenly see *your* face?
Or that when I hear *that* song, I'm not transported back to *our* old place?

As though remnants of you and me and sometimes even 'us', Aren't distributed through space and time holding everything else up?
As though shadows don't exist in darkness or stars when skies are bright?
As though when I hear your old voicemails everything isn't magically alright?

As though I don't still dot my 'i's with smiles like you showed me when we were nine?
As though I don't still use the same excuse when I'm pretending that I'm fine?
As though rain doesn't fall in droplets or manifest itself in tears?

As though my heart hasn't been haunted by the thought of you
for all these many years?

He shouted "What the fuck are we here for?"
And then, his voice disappeared.

If a cloud was as heavy as your head feels right now,
It would be raining.

It is okay to cry.

If you think about them whilst you paint/draw/write/sing,
You are probably in love with them.

I was painting today and all I could think about was you.

We stopped and started like time was no object.

I never had heroes when I was growing up,

But I didn't need them, I had my brother.

Everything he did, I learned to do.

We were an extension of each other.

As we've grown up, we've grown slightly apart,

But I still wear his hand-me-down clothes.

I look to my brother as we live our lives.

He's still my hero, I hope that he knows.

All of the words sound pretty when you say them.

Space.

Nothing is sacred and everything is,
Pancakes for breakfast, my name from your lips.

And I don't know,
How far this will go,
But life feels easier now.

Is there a god or are we all alone?
There are tears in my coffee, my friend's on the phone.

And I don't know,
Why you chose to go,
But life is difficult now.

I go to sleep so I won't fall apart,
Turn on the TV so I can't hear my heart.

And I don't know,
When this feeling will go,
But my life is still happening now.

Nothing is sacred and everything is,
Pancakes for breakfast, the space from your lips.

And I don't know,
Where I will go,
But life can be different now.

"Why are you still up?" You asked.
"In case you were." I replied.

What I found in you left me feeling lost.
So, I took a step back and prayed time would stop.
Of course, time carried on and so did my day,
But I spoke to my heart, she had something to say:
"Your life isn't fixed; it is always in flux.
Your love is worth more than a couple of bucks.
Don't settle down for someone who's just 'fine',
Find the person who sees all that truth in your eyes.
That person will know that your time and your space,
Is a delicate matter not a fist fight, not a race.
Real love is coming, it will soon be found.
That love won't be nothing, it will make you feel proud."

I felt the Earth turn when you looked at me.

I break my own heart all of the time.
You are nothing special.

We are here to paint and sing and to dance and write.
To be kind, to try hard and to look at the sky.
To hold hands and cry tears, to be together and alone.
To find a place in ourselves that feels like a home.

Life kicked him in the ass.
But he was getting better.

I took your pinkie in a promise and then you dropped my hand.
I was falling out of love and you already had.

Villanelle.

When will we be together?
We are each other's reflection.
I'm here with you, forever.

I tried to leave once, however,
You stopped me to ask the question,
When will we be together?

You called us fated, said we were tethered,
To your rainbow, I am your sun.
I'm here with you forever.

Does god make us fight for his pleasure?
I'll ask at his next resurrection.
"When will we be together?"

A new start turns final endeavour,
If the end has already begun,
When will we be together?

You're at my grave in bad weather,
You whisper with some desperation,
"When will we be together?"
I'm here, with you, forever.

When it rains,
I think I understand,
That the things that cause growth,
Are never usually planned.

I said "I think I might love you,"
You smiled, "That'd be okay."

Idle hands and idle minds tell love stories all the time.

One day you'll grow old,
With the weight of a thousand hearts,
Tied to your own,
And it will be worth it.

<u>I have a friend.</u>

I have a friend; I think she's fallen from the stars.
I looked into her eyes; she's travelled very far.
There are constellations on her face and on her arms,
She holds meteors in her palms.

I have a friend; I think she's going to change the world.
She's under pressure but she turns stress into pearls.
She's had a dream ever since she was a little girl.
I hope I'm there when it unfurls.

I have a friend who must belong in a fairy tale.
When there's a storm, she's sure to sing about the gale.
She walks into rain and tries to rescue all of the snails.
She sees diamonds where there is hail.

I have a friend who's fierce, she never seems to cave.
She stayed kind even when she was given less than she gave,
And if you ask her how she got to be so brave,
She'll say: the ocean can't fear waves.

I have a friend who fell and thought that she was broken,
For a while she thought the world moved in slow motion,
But when the dark crept in, she found a way to focus,
She found strength in her emotion.

I have a friend; I think that she might know it all.
She's always intentional but effortlessly cool,
And when you stand by her, she makes you feel like you're ten
feet tall.
She thinks reality's for fools.

And in my friends, I found a strength I didn't know was there.
I found hope and peace and trust and new ways I could care.
My friends are teachers, artists, dancers, soulmates, rare.
I feel their love even when they aren't there.

She was the ocean.
I was in love.

I know that all I said was,
"Goodbye"
But I hope that it sounded like,
"I love you"

When my sister sings, her voice fills the whole house,
So, I used to like being home alone.
But now I've moved out, and she isn't around,
I call her and she sings through the phone.

I know that I have not been the same,
Since the first time, I heard you say my name.

I spend my wishes wishing I could spend more time with you.

Twenty-Eight / Decades

Your perfume on my pillow and my hand in your hair,
We talked 'til way past midnight. We were tired, didn't care.
I learned about your family and you asked me about mine.
We fell asleep in denim with our bodies intertwined.

When we woke up, we ate pancakes with ice cream,
We drank our coffee slowly and you asked me what it means,
When we say that we're friends, but it feels like something more,
And how can this be *nothing*, when our feelings are so raw?

I looked at you for a second, then I looked down to the ground.
I smiled and shrugged and said, "I really like when you're around?"
I told you that I liked you like "I've liked nobody else."
Then I stayed really quiet hoping you felt what I felt.

You looked at me and laughed and then you sighed and smiled and swore,
You took me by the waist, kissed me, and we fell to the floor.
The ice cream was left melting and the coffee going cold,
When we looked at each other, the whole world turned to gold.

We were twenty-eight back then and decades since have passed.
It seems so strange to think we ever thought we'd never last.
Now every year, on June the third, we buy an ice cream cake,
And celebrate the fact that we are more than "just good mates".

"Well, have you ever seen a sunset?"

"Yeah?"

"Then of course you've been in love."

Today.

Today I'm growing old, alone,
But the day is altogether young,
And I know tomorrow is on my side,
So long as I get up and try.

The trying will be hard,
But some days, they will come easy,
And some people will stay,
And some people will leave me.

I've been left before,
And I've been the one to leave,
I need to work on loving,
I'm still learning how to grieve.

I like cyclical endings,
And poems that rhyme neatly,
But growing up and growing old,
Don't always come so easy.

Our love's a natural disaster.

A Self-Portrait.

If you know who I am, can you please let me know,
Because I feel so lost. I don't know where to go.
Forward seems scary but backwards does too.
The sun is surely shining but I still feel blue.

Maybe one day, it won't matter the weather.
The sky will be grey but I will feel better.
Maybe, sometime, I will find my direction,
And my body – my mind – won't feel like a question.

Sometimes a bone has to be broken for it to be set in place again.
I guess it must be the same with a heart?

Gas Station Flowers.

I picked you up some flowers on the way back from the store.
I would've got them in there but they cost a dollar more,
Than the guy who's on the corner of the gas station off Mark's,
And I might've added wild ones when I cut across the park.

But I know you like them thrifty and I know you like them
wild,
I know you'd rather have the dollar than the flowers neatly
styled,
Because the dollars add up quickly and the bills have to get
paid,
And it's been a couple years since we last got away.

I'd been saving my spare change in the glovebox in my car,
So, I *could* buy you flowers and we could put them in a vase,
And I know I could've drawn a picture of a flower or bouquet,
And that you would've thought that that was *more* than just
okay.

But I'd been thinking of how you love me, and how I love you
too,
And how I'd never seen a flower a more perfect shade of you.

I don't know much about falling but I don't think that it's supposed to hurt.

The other day you asked who I write about,
And I didn't know how to say "You."
So instead, I said "Everyone, nobody, someone"
But I think that you already knew.
You shrugged and said, "I'm someone."
I laughed and said, "Yes, that is true."
But I guess I was wrong because you carried on,
And said, "No, really, I want to know who?"

What If The Love Is Never Ours?

What if the love is never ours,
And the good guys never win,
What if the ending isn't happy,
And the poets never sing?

What if the music's cut off early,
And I still can't dance the dance,
What if the whole world ends tomorrow,
And I still haven't been to France?

What if the clocks get stuck at midnight,
What if the sun forgets to rise,
What if we all forget about sadness,
And no tears fall from our eyes?

What if I go to sleep this evening,
And when I wake up something's wrong,
What if I don't paint another painting,
What if the ladybirds are all gone?

What if paradise has fallen,
What if hope is just a lie,
What if we burn down all our forests,
And forget we are alive?

What if I am never happy,
Because I'm so afraid to hurt,
What if I don't write that story,
Because I overthink the words?

What if trees all become shiny,
And thus, impossible to climb,
What if I die before I'm ready,
Before I write the perfect rhyme?

What if the world's already over,
And none of this is real,
What if we are all just robots,
Who've been programmed how to feel?

What if Doctor Who gets cancelled,
What if Rock and Roll does die,
What if life always feels this heavy,
Or Peter Pan could never fly?

What if I spend so much time thinking,
That I forget to go outside,
What if I think the love is gone,
And then? My heart beats one more time.

The light in my room is warm.
Your side of the bed is cold.
I'm picturing you inside of my head,
Because you are not there to hold.

Friendship is my favourite kind of poetry.

He told you that he'd never been given flowers before,
So, you left and ran straight to the store.
You picked a bouquet and a bottle of wine,
When you got home, he so nearly cried.
It's Valentine's Day and sure, you are both alone,
But you're more than just friends. You are each other's home.

Unhappy Lovers.

Unhappy lovers in the ruins of a heart,
The best of intentions long from where they start.
Withered "I love you"s tangled beneath sheets,
Doubtfulness disguised in desperate belief.

Little fulfilment is compromised for a home,
Craving togetherness - though apart they have grown.
A safety net is still a net, and a net is a trap,
Wasted minutes on a clock, careless drips from a tap.

Waiting is a chore. Anticipation is a curse.
But a life without the latter is infinitely worse,
So, the two unhappy lovers untether their hearts,
Because when one becomes two, then their lives can restart.

The shape of your absence is too familiar to me.

One Day I'll Have A House.

One day, I'll have a house with brown pigeon hole drawers,
And a lunchbox full of coppers to hold open the doors.
I'll use a mini fridge as a table and old tiles in place of coasters,
And I'll host all of my friends on a way too tiny sofa.

I'll have mismatched cutlery and lots of hand thrown mugs,
And I'll let the lawn get overgrown so it's more fun for the bugs.
There will always be ice cream and lasagne and baked beans,
And there'll always be a spare bed and an extra set of keys.

I'll host a murder mystery and set an easel up outside,
I'll have a whole wall full of photographs that everyone will sign.
I'll leave some bricks exposed so that I can feel the cold,
And I'll dance in the kitchen even when I am alone.

When I lay the table, there'll be a spare place at the head.
There'll be a whole room just for painting and I'll have a Murphy bed.
In the porch, there'll be a sketchbook. There'll be one in every room,
And in the garden, there's a bench so I can sit up with the moon.

All my coats live on a hat rack and have sharpies in their pockets,
There's a toy box in the corner full of juggling balls and bop-it.

I keep a towel by the back door for when I'm dancing in the rain,
And there are always loads of paintings still waiting to be framed.

When it's my turn to host Christmas everyone brings their own chair,
We all eat in the living room and play drunken solitaire.
There's a crown hung on the door, like a wreath – more like a star,
And the Christmas tree is handmade from the bonnet of a car.

The house always smells like fresh bread, or oil paint or both,
And in my imagination, it's surrounded by a moat.
All my plants have names and they're usually from books.
Some were quite expensive but their prices, overlooked.

There's a toolbox full of letters and another full of tools,
And a third one full of coloured chalk for drawing on the walls.
When I first move in, I'll draw a moustache on the mirror,
To make me laugh when I walk past to the kitchen to make dinner.

I don't pay the rent because the house belongs to me,
I bought it outright, selling paintings, now I wake up by the sea.
There's an empty cola bottle filled with flowers from my walk,
One day that house will be real but for now it's all just talk.

My heart is on fire but so is the world,
I guess I chose the wrong time to fall for the girl.

Love is ordinary and that is brilliant.

<u>Greta.</u>

The world you wished to live and breathe,
Is the world that's been laid out for me,
And I wish that you were here to live it too.

The day you dreamed would come around,
When you could be out, standing proud,
Where you could be a girl who loved a girl.

Where you can steal a look and look again,
Have a story with a happy end,
And have a family you know will love you back.

Where you can hold her hand and walk the street,
And wake up together in the sheets,
And feel less fear when you should be feeling love.

It was you, you know, who paved the way,
I think about it every day,
How you were brave so I could live in peace.

I'm safe here and that's thanks to you,
But there is still more work to do,
So, I'll be brave just like you showed me how.

There is iron in your blood that came from the stars,
And people in your heart who made you who you are.

Love is in it all.

Time feels richer when I am with you.

If she was a raincloud then,
She was also the sun.

A Sunday, In The Fall.

I wanted to make you breakfast but you had woken early.
I stumbled to the kitchen whilst my vision was still blurry.
You were in my t-shirt and the radio was on,
With a wooden spoon for a microphone, I watched you sing along.

I asked if you'd made coffee or if I could make one for you.
You kissed me on the forehead, passed your mug and whispered "Thank you."
I asked what you were making and how come you were awake,
You said you'd had a nightmare so you got up and baked a cake.

It's half five in the morning, on a Sunday, in the fall.
We're breaking down your nightmare – or the parts that you recall.
We're eating cake for breakfast, on the counter, by the stove.
If this is our life forever, I can't wait for growing old.

We are lonely *and* we are loved.

Let us write about all of the things that feel impossible to say,
And stay up, holding each other, until night turns to day.

One day your last name will also be my own,
But for now, it's just the password that unlocks my phone.

The Poem About Stargazing.

We sit on the rooftop and look at the stars,
You try to show me a meteor but it flies by too fast.
You're sad I didn't see it but I think it's funny,
I say that it's okay, "It's what they do, honey."
You say "That's sad. Why can't gold always trail through the sky,
Like a Vincent van Gogh you get to see every night?"
I say "It is… or it can be, if you like,
You just have to squint and hold tears in your eyes."

You tell me that's sad again and I say "That's true,
But so are shooting stars and they're beautiful too.
They all burn out and they die on their own.
They make you smile crazy wide but they'll never know."
"How on Earth is that beautiful?" you ask and I say:
"Well, you think it's sad but you're smiling away.
See, something that's sad doesn't have to be so,
If you change the meaning of where that thing goes.

If the star isn't dying then death's no destination.
It's just carrying your wish to a very safe haven.
And yes, the star's gone and no, it didn't see you smile,
But you took something alone and were a friend for a while."
It was just a story about a star in the sky,
But you believed it so fully there were tears in your eyes.
You squinted, looked up, saw the trails made of gold,
And said, "Doesn't thinking like this make you feel fucking old?"

I nodded and smiled, wrapped my cold arms around you,
And whispered, "Beauty brings sadness but vice versa too."
You tell me that's sad again and I say "Yes, but it's pretty,
And it's really okay, our hearts have the capacity.
We make wishes for stars who are running out of time,
We don't just tell people we love them; we make our words
rhyme.
We cry over characters that we read about in books,
And throw dinner parties for friends even though we can't
cook."

That night held so much but my favourite part,
Was when you looked at me, sighed and started to laugh.
You said "I get that it's pretty and not *only* sad,
But I really wish that you saw that star when I had."
It was my turn to ask why it mattered so much,
And you lent in so close that, once again, our arms touched.
You said "It's just, that there are so many stars in the sky,
How could we know which one caught the other's eye?

Unless it happened to be shooting and we *both* pointed and
gasped,
And how if we did, we would probably laugh.
But then, we would think 'How low are the chances,
That the same single star would captivate and command us?'
And how beautiful it would be if we knew then for sure,
That my wish would stay - forever - with yours?"
I said "Oh, that is sad. Or it would be if this wasn't true:
I didn't see the shooting star because I was looking at you."

I said "We don't need wishes to know that we're safe,
Or that you and I end up in the very same place."
But since it matters that much then I know what we'll do,
We can watch the stars tomorrow. I'll look at them and not
you."
And we did for a while, every night for a week.
Until on the last night when you started to speak.
You said "Okay, we can go. I've seen all the stars that I need.
It's hard to focus on them when you're next to me."

So now when we hear that there are showers of stars,
We turn to each other and once again laugh,
Because we see the stars in the day and the night,
And we don't need wishes to know we're alright.
But still, we find ourselves watching from the field 'cross the
street,
Because finding all the stars friends is one heck of a feat.
And hey, it would still be cool to be able to say,
That we saw the same shooting star on the very same day.

We've known each other for a million years.
I knew I loved you before I knew *I* was real.

We drank chocolate milk out of champagne flutes and danced
the Waltz in our pyjamas,
I stood on your feet by accident. You said, "It's a good job
you're a charmer."
We ordered pizza on the phone from a flyer through the door.
And I swear to god, Emilia, I've never loved you more.

<u>Meet me where the fireflies live.</u>

Meet me where the fireflies live, in the forest, near the creek.
It's in the middle of nowhere we find the home that we seek.
There's nobody around but we still seem to whisper.
We pretend we're somewhere fancy. I call you 'Miss' you call
me 'Mister'.

"How can you see something when nobody else thinks it's
there?"
You ask me absentmindedly as you play with my hair.
I turn around to face you and ask what you're thinking about.
You say "Nothing in particular." Your voice is full of doubt.

I stood up, held out my hand and asked if you'd like to dance.
I said "We'll run away and find the lost. We'll start in Paris,
France."
You laughed and then you nodded, "That's where all the lost
things go,
And when we're bored of France we can leave and go to
Rome."

So that was that, decided. We were off to find the lost.
The invisible, the imaginary, old pirate ships, the lot.
Of course, we didn't really. We were just two kids in love.
We fell asleep tangled together whilst the stars danced up
above.

When we woke, the grass was cold and the dew had settled in.
The fireflies had gone and now the birds were chiming in.
At first, the world was too much for our very sleepy minds,
But once we'd woken up we knew the sun was on our side.

117

We talked for a while longer before we said goodbye.
I said I had a quarter and I'd call at half past five.
You held me by the waist. I picked my coat up off the floor.
Back then you gave me butterflies, we had peace, now we have war.

The real world is the one that accepts you.
It's okay to spend more of your time there than anywhere else.

In hindsight, I think it was love.

I'll always walk the long way home if that means I can walk with you.

I feel like I know you without having to talk,
And maybe that's the realest kind of love out of them all.

Caffeine doesn't keep me awake. Thinking of you does.

They didn't fit in anywhere but they also didn't stick out,
So, for the longest time, their head was full of doubt.
They didn't realise that they'd have to define themself this much,
And every time somebody asked, it was like a heavy punch.
There are so many questions from the world and from themself,
That they imagine bottled thoughts and stack them on a shelf.
They don't need to have the answers and they don't have to give them away.
The only thing that matters is living life, today.

We fell in spring and we wilted in autumn.

Out Loud.

She fell in love with a girl and she said it out loud.
The world didn't end, there were no final bows.

She fell in love with a girl and the girl loved her back.
They lived happily ever after. Queer joy is a fact.

The Tree Grows.

We took a walk in the forest and sat under a tree,
We carved a heart in the trunk with a 'C' and a 'G',

You turned my baseball cap backwards and lifted my chin,
You kissed me so softly but I still felt you grin.

You said I was blushing. I joked I had "No idea why,"
We both started to laugh and then looked up at the sky,

We stayed there until dark, we had no other plans.
You imagined our futures from the lines on our hands.

It was only for a season but it was as real as anything,
When you had packed your bags, is when it started to sting.

I kissed you in the doorway and you took off my hat,
You said you'd see me in six months and then you would give
it back.

A Sequel To The Stargazing Poem.

When the world ends, we'll dream about Mars.
We'll sit on the rooftop, eat pizza, watch stars.
The asteroids will strike until then we'll hold back our tears.
Our future's in the past. We've got minutes not years.

There's a broadcast called 'The End'. It's sponsored by
McCains,
Where celebrities perform to try and counteract their shame.
They're waiting for a text with their boarding pass details,
And RSVP-ing with their dinner time meals.

Our song will start playing. We'll get up to dance,
But we'll both be so tired I'll just sway in your arms.
We'll take polaroids of each other that we know won't survive.
We'll caption them with Sharpie 'The Only Lovers Left Alive.'

The sirens will start blaring and panic will endure.
There'll be thousands of thoughts that we'll try to ignore.
You'll try and make it less scary, "It's just a huge shooting
star."
We'll die here tonight but we both start to laugh.

We'll close our eyes tight, and make our last wishes on Earth.
And decide we get three - that's the least we'd deserve.
I'll wish that it will be quick and that it won't hurt,
And that there is an afterlife and it's better than Earth.

I'll rest my head on your shoulder and whisper "Goodbye,"
You'll tell me to stop as tears fall from our eyes.
You'll say you wished you were an Artist, or a Poet, or the
Pope,
Because then this might've been beautiful. You might've found
hope.

I'll say "If they find *this* beautiful, they must be far too alone."
You'll smile and say "It's stupid, we're being wiped out by a
stone."
I'll choke on my milkshake and try to hide my laugh,
"Wiped out by a stone!? You're right. That is daft."

We'll sit there together strangely happy and sad,
And swear we'll still get to finish the plans that we have.
The dust fills our lungs. It hurts so much when we cry.
Then the asteroid strikes and, the lovers? We'll die.

When you try to turn people into poems every day,
You realise that there's something in everyone,
That's impossible to explain.

Printed in Great Britain
by Amazon

32284390R00078